"Maria Vasquez Boyd's poetry collection *The Weight of Recogntion* begins with the line, "At birth his tiny heart was replaced with a rabbits' heart." It is a jolting line given her disclosure of a heart condition. (All is better and getting better.) This is no lament but the words of a woman whose heart is, "the shape of a mourning dove/hunkered down in the wind. ... the shape of fists/that pummel locked doors." This is a poet alive in the world serving notice. "Gentle hearts bend to carry parched souls/Back to the ground where desperate journeys begin. ... Hearts divided between two worlds who forge trails of tears/ and two paragraphs in history books." While "Pragmatic men motionless/prefer sickness to the cure," Boyd is, "The woman who decorates her forearms with henna instead of razor blades/considers flesh filled loops and spirals/like a walking hieroglyph awaiting translation." In Whisper Song, one of many gems in this collection, Boyd asks, "What offerings does one make to a soul whose journey is long and uncertain?" The answer comes in the last line of the collection "... she leaned over the/cockpit/ and thanked the pilot for the ride."

-Jose Faus is a founding member of the Latino
Writers Collective and sits on the boards of the
Latino Writers Collective, UMKC Friends of the
Library, Charlotte Street Foundation and is
president of the board of The Writers Place.

"In *The Weight of Recognition*, Maria Vasquez Boyd indulges us in the multiple meanings of the human heart and the bitter-sweet weight of living and the passage of time. She brings attention to the most minute aspects of love in "the simplicity of synchronized wings and love duets." In this collection the heart becomes its own world and we are entranced in the beauty and mystery of it. She elegantly captures the varied nuances of simply being alive."

-Diane Vogel Ferri, Author of *Everything is Rising*

"Maria Vasquez Boyd's *The Weight of Recognition* is a fascinating poetic quest in which the poet asks whether the self (the "shifting mask" in the mirror) can be located by faith or doubt, through her heritage or self-portrait in "slow paint," in romantic imagination or mundane experience (like mending pocket holes). Its chief recurring image is the human heart— like a fist, a mouth, a mourning dove "hunkered down" in wind; beating to the "pizzicato" of a clock; related to the monarch butterfly that the poet places inside her shirt. Boyd's collection features fresh imagery, honest longing, highly original use of language, and—best of all—an epiphany of self-knowing."

-Linda M. Lewis, *This Swirling Largesse*

THE WEIGHT OF RECOGNITION

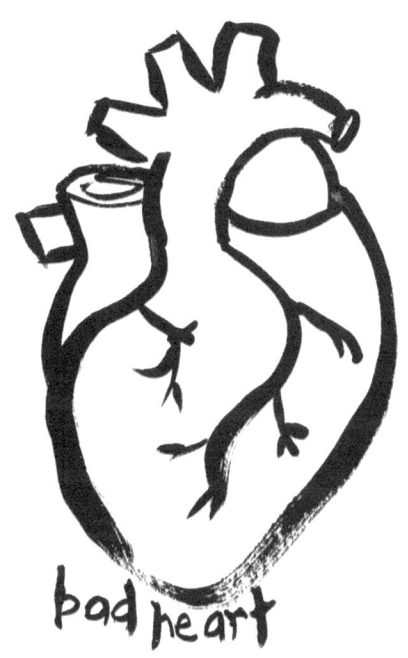

bad heart

POEMS BY MARIA VASQUEZ BOYD

Spartan
Press

Spartan Press

Kansas City, MO

spartanpress.com

Spartan
Press

Copyright © Maria Vasquez Boyd, 2022

First Edition: 1 3 5 7 9 10 8 6 4 2

ISBN: 978-1-958182-08-6

LCCN: 2022940194

Author photo and cover image: Maria Vasquez Boyd

Acknowledgments:

Many encouraged this chapbook, thank you to Jump Start Art, Sharon Eiker, Jason Ryberg, Spartan Press, Elizabeth Andersen, Miguel M. Morales, Missouri Poet Laureate Maryfrances Wagner, Kansas Poet Laureate Huascar Medina, Diane Vogel Ferri, Linda M. Lewis and José Faus.

My gratitude and love to Terri, Toni, Nick, Natalie, Andrew, Caleb, Luke, Rose, Moni, Paul, Jen, Becky and Nicolette.

Special thanks to the editors of these publications where some of the poemss in this collection first appeared:

"The Virgin's Children," *Everyday Things,*
"Our Obsessive Desire to Understand Why," *Everyday
    Things,*
"11:11," *Toasted Cheese,*
"Pagare II Prezzo," *Present Magazine,*
"Ellipsis," Johnson County Library, *Poem in your Pocket,*
"Lovers and Other Dark Horses," *Present Magazine,*
"River, America Now and Here," traveling art/poetry
    exhibit Eric Fischl,
"Colla Voce," *Present Magazine,*
"Ukulele and Color Fields," *Kansas City Star,*
"10,000 Lies," *Primera Página: Poetry from the Latino
    Heartland*
"Windowpane," *Primera Página: Poetry from the Latino
    Heartland*

TABLE OF CONTENTS

To Luna, Scout, and Mr. Boyd, siempre te amo

10,000 Lies

No one knew

At birth his tiny heart was replaced with a rabbit's heart
Exotic and furious beats resonate
as the rabbit heart snuggles in his chest

Large clouds form letters into words that are ignored
Shivering monarchs migrant clockwise
as weeping icons wave

But the hand that touches another
senses fear
and possibilities

Pragmatic men
motionless
prefer sickness to the cure

And 5 drunken writers
collapse in a heap of jumbled words
only to hold their heart
and wonder what happened

11:11

The charm of a heart
is that it appears to be heart-shaped
But it's not

In fact
it resembles
the shape of a
mourning dove
hunkered down
in the wind

It's the shape of fists
that pummel locked doors

Or
the shape of a mouth
that murmurs,
no one loves me

Hopeless romantics
and children
release hearts
from folded paper
with scissors

But the disappointment
of an imperfect heart

underlines an angry truth

that things never turn

out the way you want

Alibi

A woman's lips
Represent the power of seduction

Possibilities exist in the minds of men

Leaving their calling card
on lips and skin

Women, like thieves in the dark
imprint the lives they touch

Wiping away the lipstick
erases that particular moment
with that particular person

The memory tossed away like a tissue

Alpha

We, and when I say we, I mean me
have forgotten the flutter of shiny lemon-colored aspen
leaves in a struggle to remain attached to a living organism

We, and when I say we I mean me
have forgotten music river sound
of water from mountains
too old to reveal their true age

During a hike, a round imperfect stone imbedded in sand
waited 25 years, no a thousand years to reveal itself to me

It glows in my hand as I roll it forward over and over
It leaves no trace minerals or mica, sand, or organism,
no memory from its tenure in ground

Layers of history and time
press tightly with boiling sand
a few million years ago,
Shaped and reshaped
The remains of volcanoes
in a tumbling world
of unfortunate timing

But now this object
this black stone has taken its place
Inside another stone

Within a smaller stone
Inside an even smaller stone

Is nothing something?
In its nothingness, we, I mean me,
Rejoice in its secrets
In possibilities

Apogee

When the moon passes between the earth and the sun
Something better will arrive

The simplicity of synchronized wing beats and love duets
Sadden the pilot who seeks calm in wind tunnels
He believes private fumblings and bumping shadows
    too obscene

The quickness of motion suspends his mind
Flapping his arms, he believes a propeller is a wing in
    rotation

A soul falls earth bound through wind, sound, and
    cerulean blue sky
Waiting patiently for nothingness

Borderland

The fate of a child reveals itself through shattered
mirrors
The weft and warp of destructive
hate-infused fabric
wound tightly

We are borderless butterflies
Native aliens
Hearts divided between two worlds
who forge trails of tears
and two paragraphs in history books

Ghosts from another time
Si estamos juntos

Caesar's Woman

The top notes of perfume

orange blossom
and Egyptian jasmine

suffocate thoughts
on his pillow

Perhaps she would stay
feel the glow of heavy objects
on a bumpy night

Smile
Chant
Promise

But on this evening

The prediction of meteror showers
toss in sad skies
throwing its weight
against the door
like angry dogs

Calando

The expectation of a different outcome
Through an unchanged sequence of events
Is like a dog who chases cars

When flesh and bone collide against scraping metal
The sad faces of curious children look upon a beloved pet

A dog that chased away the quiet fears of children at night
And nipped at their fingers expecting sticky candy and fruit
 as a reward

But children are curious about death
The dog looks as though he is sleeping

Yet the dog did not move
And the children did not move

In the silence of death
They will remember this day

As they are certain to remember
The days of Mothers and Fathers
The days of Brothers and Sisters
The stillness of loss in one another

Colla Voce

A river thick with the sediment
of a forgotten sea

carves soil
from trees
tethered to earth

Unhappy to flow
from one direction
the river
swirls in circles
till it lassoes
an island

And on this private island
of hollow trees
and owls

inverted bottles
of amber
and green glass
attach to earth
like hearts in purgatory

A person of magic
happily discovers
glass that shimmers

and sprouts

from a well-tended garden

And swallows the disbelief

Of that moment

In mid-air

Compass

We are looking for one thing
The direction you take is determined by the weather

When the cold arrived, I went North
Growth, light, decay is the life blood of nature

I touched the old shadow of a mountain
The energy made visible in snow and ice
Hand to earth

The sound of stacked ice cracks
A trail of broken lines start and stop

We fixate on patterns that retain an after image in a single
  moment

Only a tiny region in the center of the eye can see
sharply
A mind can be tricked into believing what it sees

Gentle hearts bend to carry parched souls
Back to the ground where desperate journeys begin

Divine Touch of Gods

Points in motion suggest movement
Line implies edge

Follow the contours of an amethyst
Turn it over in your hand

Crushing

Till particles imitate stars in the galaxy
that cannot escape the weight of its own gravity

Thus rendering matter into darkness

Elixir

That elusive butterfly of a heart
landed gently touching you

Perhaps startled at first,
A thought bubble announced,
"I am in love!"

That proclamation uttered over and over
to your friends
to your family
and even to the cat who scratched his head
and thought, "That's crazy."

Then under a tangerine moon, you know.
"This is the one."

A graceful dance began.
One that defines your life together,
your dreams together,

And the path you take together.
Like delicate butterflies
Touching the sky.

Ellipsis

Wooden floors
uneven as a drunk
who blows a kiss
at no one

the one who
is not in love
with a drunk blowing kisses

In rare moments of sobriety
desires another drink

He believes
funny people
mask pain with humor

Thus drunks become
increasingly funnier
the more they drink

Living life in a blur
he continues
scattering particles
of memory

Like a sweeping ghost

Epiphany

Bodies float in circular motion
trapped by whirlpools

A gifted individual wears sunglasses
in the moonlight and becomes invisible

Lying in a trance on the bed
you form a backward "C"

Pleas no longer penetrate your ears
and cannot accept the pitch and weight of sad words
trapped like balloons in angry skies

And so it doesn't matter if you say it doesn't exist

The letter "A" held at arms-length
cannot cure the imbalance of a person
who views it with metronome eyes

The woman who decorates her forearms with henna
instead of razor blades
considers flesh-filled loops and spiral
like a walking hieroglyph awaiting translation

Following Water

The unattainable beauty
of spider web doilies with translucent beads
in delicate suspension,

remind you of the fragile moments
you listen for signals

Only to find the sound of metal on metal
inside your head,
that carries the responsibility of failure

Harlow's Monkey

Hiding in a closet under racks of skirts and pants
that define who I am and what I am not

Some things will never be worn again
I am no longer that person

Those who love you will raise an eyebrow
when you emerge from the quiet the loneliness

But you will speak another time
this day is for pounding hearts

And soulless gestures
Brothers with seizures

And birds seeking warmth

Lit

What do burning angels smell like?
Milestones and miracles happen

Stones
glow in the dark

Former drug addicts and alcoholics share
euphoric recall
Like recovering attorneys
who sit in a circle
and utter mea culpas

The intellectual sits
Cross-legged in his tent and giggles
Recorded basketball tournaments
delight him like porn
He deals in brain matter
that is to say, he thinks

Pages fill with loops and circles
to represent what can't be said aloud

And an eye gouged out
records an afterimage
of wrestling shadows
covered in ash

Lovers and Other Dark Horses

Love no one fully
but believe in delicate good luck
and bare whispers

Lateral thinkers learn the only way is up

In a city of angry men
ready for revolution,
women of the romanticos dress in the dark

In that glorious distress
a heart beats to the pizzicato drip of a clock

Helpless dancers
in blurred photographs
reveal nothing

While others talk to heaven
in a perfect light

Stars in the same galaxy
rotate clockwise
in opposite directions
like fighting cats

Our Obsessive Desire to Understand Why

In the cool
whiteness of this space

I smile
I listen in broken syllables
and fragments

I am invisible
I recognize human faces as less human
I am a shifting mask in the mirror
I masquerade as ordinary

I look at myself and I am not pleased
I yearn for invincibility in this temporary body

My cold and impermeable eyes
have become an outward reflection of who I am

I dream the power of birds

Outline

Stars scattered the skies over a black beach
Mutilated sea turtles would not prevent him
from lying on his back on Mexican sand

He begged her to stay with him on the beach
Magic spilled from his fingertips
And filled her pockets

He traced constellations on the back of her neck
Stars tumbled over her vertebrae

The words she spoke contained his name or so he thought
He rocked her between his legs and asked, Do you believe?

And in her quiet hunger, she believes

Oval Storms in September

And still they come

Where land and sky converge
an original thinker
with eyes the color of olives
search cloud-ravaged heavens
for dark stars

Only to find a nocturnal ghost
who rolls and tumbles in a small bed

Wary of two- fisted heart agreements
yet admires what negative space surrounds,

That other blankness of the unknown takes form

Like a watch with broken arms
pointing to a significant event
occurring at a precise moment

Pagare Il Prezzo
To Pay the Price

A harried bachelor
prepares dinner
in his underwear
mindful of peppers and mangoes

A hand touches his forearm
thus confirms his existence

Sleepless nights
a Rubik's cube of possibilities
unfinished business
And life on tiptoes

So now then
No one will object to human needs

In the velvet silence
clumsy acrobats perform at night

In a city of cloud-pasted skies
and hippies
he gave her the ocean

Footprints dissolve in saltwater
Eucalyptus trees
drop wooden buttons
in Japanese gardens

And
an idealist admires
a harried bachelor
who prepares dinner
in his underwear
mindful of peppers and mangoes

Petit Four

The tiny frosted cake sits delicately on your plate
The pink napkin upon your lap begins to curl

Scolding yourself for eating the damn thing
You wash it away with the champagne from your plastic cup

River

Touch the green murky water of the Little Blue River
Discover the void of blue stolen by bluebirds that
    point toward happiness

Where anticipation of a perigee full moon,
    the brightest in fourteen years
could not be found on an indigo night and
    disappointment followed

Like a claim once made by an ancient sea that existed,

Long before the sound of trains crisscrossing
    the West Bottoms

Long before a mysterious mound of earth held tightly
    a secret in Northeast

Long before the tiny minds of primitives with plastic
    currency
began casting cups and bottles afloat
down the green murky water of the Little Blue River

Self Portrait with Slow Paint

Step into negative space
between shadow trees

The infra sound of elephants
travels faster than the speed of sound

Thus form
shapes in response to wind

Live close to the ground

Trees connect their roots to other trees

Feelings follow behavior

The sad man at night
is made immortal
by a woman who touches his forehead
to clear the unforgiving aroma of another

And in this discovery
he is grateful for what others reject

Spectre

You touch my face with fingerless hands
held tightly clenched in pockets with holes

The nothingness of holes
You cannot weep for the loss of something you
    cannot hold

Like the love of a sweet woman who sadly examined
exact holes neatly cut in each pocket

Who with a sturdy needle wove invisible thread
into the fabric
and out of the nothingness of holes

Sunday Morning

You touch the necklace
with the silver crucifix
and laugh

What a cruel joke
to demonstrate a belief
in hope and faith
and not fully believe

Love is a soul sucker
not intended for you

We smile for hidden cameras
in public places
and hold hands with tarnished rings

We vow not to die alone
but we do anyway

Such a bitter ending
for fine clothes
and humble furniture parceled out to strangers
unaware of the careless history of raised voices

And fists at that exact table
now delivered to foreign homes

Talisman

Magically thinking aloud reminds you of mirrors in a
    funhouse
Layers of patterns repeat and obscure the original object

Afflicted and feverish, the linen shirt absorbs his sweat
Fingers spurt precise words onto paper
Subtle barometric pressure shifts between sentences

The constant white noise heard in his other life is
    temporarily ceased

In his best Southern drawl,
He is desired
absolved
shiny

Shared secrets and rhetoric resurface in prose

Refined intellectual and older
A petition raced in his mind
seeking infinite joy
and her admiration

Ten of Coins

What is written in your heart
when your eyes flutter?

In the world of secrets
finding love
hiding love
chasing cloud shadows on pavement

Public hands clasp in prayer
ask for strength to resist exposed skin

Mouth petal
soft and eager
In private elegance
touch

An attentive woman forges iron into
organic shapes

Together
but not together

Light fills a crack in the door

The Collapse of Stars

Heavenly bodies are thousands of degrees
hotter than the stars they circle

A visiting nurse
adjusts expressions of death
into a pleasing smile

Men from the East Bay
search with manic eyes
for exact words

While a bearded magician in Japanese gardens
punched holes in the air
She's there but not really there

Cut away the third beat of a heart beating
Rub away the pulse of sadness
under the tilt of a smiling moon

Swat it away
like the hum of a mosquito
on an indigo night

The Other Side of Saturn

Shepherd moons orbit around one another
with Triton traveling backwards around Neptune

But the expansion of the universe is not slowing down
In fact, it's speeding up

Serenity lies in a brown bottle
tossed in your direction

Speak boldly
Speak low
Whisper what you seek to the thief of time

Everything moves outward and accelerates
when circles travel in circular motion

An object moves outward
as it accelerates

The Positive Aspects of Negative Space

The negative space of letters and sound fill with
    darkness

The space above
The space below
The space between

The curious function of brain hemispheres
The shape of English walnuts,
Cross over inner lives and floating worlds

Fingertips trace what is not "there"
Exact perception suspends time

The Secret of Motionless Movement

Ambient light exposed each muted thinker
The unscripted touch of her finger
circles his skin

As she marks each freckle and fold
the other women in his life become oblique

His heart, private and secure
expands to include her

He once joked that rain conditioned a response
a desire for her like Pavlov's dog

He smiles at her handprint
left behind in the shower
He happily wears shirts imprinted with her scent

At night
silhouettes of his life become distant in the dark

The Virgin's Children

Now we are civilized
We have lost a part of our old knowledge
We live a quiet life

Born under the sign of rain
An angel of light appears
Giving light to dark spirits
And widowed midwives

We have forgotten our gods

Earth
Air
Water
Sun

No one tells us why we do what we do

Tiberias

Thirsty men linger long enough
to listen for red song birds sing exact notes
in lightning storms

Those who seek holy water
in sacred spaces
boldly sit before a congregation
holding hands with lovers
and other dangerous people

While others smash apples in forbidden gardens
from an angle of elevation
where spindly trees shine in the rain
and peek into windows
like voyeurs
watching silhouettes in silent devotion

Woven tapestries depict
the faithful who know more
about slipping into Eden
Than the stains of bitter Christians

Topography/Touching Face

A pocket stuffed with money
equals emotional return

Men with muted fingertips
read flesh like obscure language

While others use mirrors to deflect objects in their path

Once a mad elephant was hung from a bridge
during the turn of the century to correct bad behavior
That'll teach him

The woman who pretends to be deaf in a room full of men
opens her eye to the one
soft and generous
who wraps himself in fingerprints
and weeps

Trilogy I

Few people know
yet condone the addiction

With ease, she slips in and out of lives

An angry lover
on one side of the French door
detects another
on the other side of the French door

As he unfolds beneath her
She traces concentric circles on his thigh
her careless signature on an unpaid loan

Ukuleles and Color Fields

My friend loves women

With his crooked smile
and crazy dog hair
he performs solos for me

One eye perpetually dilated
he paints landscapes of the women he loves

Skin folds and auburn hair reveal faraway places
softened by light and exotic fauna

Paintings surround him like folded maps
Atmospheric landscapes
moist with morning hues
appear drowsy

Like a woman
head slightly tipped
allowing her nightgown
to slip from her shoulders

Venationes

He should never have bothered it

The black snake climbed the enormous oak
Young girls noticed its movement and squealed
Mothers clutched their children and moved toward it

He would prove to her how brave her daddy could be
In her eyes, he would save her a thousand times

Her father's hands once kind, now pulled the snake from
    its grip
In slow motion, vertebrae struck the massive tree
Limp and dying yet he continued to beat the snake

With a sense of duty and arrogance, he searched the
    crowd
only to find his daughter's eye between her fingers

He should never have bothered it

By his fatherly actions, his soul becomes delicate and
    cursed
Frantic longings in his black heart remain ignored

In his peripheral vision, he is unloved by his wife
To his daughter, he resides as a haunting silhouette
Now he pleads as his family quietly place their lives in
boxes and cartons carried out the front door

Spoiled laundry and vodka bottles outline his life
In those familiar and private moments
he held invisible conversations in the Midwest breeze

As if in a trance, he spelled out her name waving his arms
    in the air

Tangled in unsecured pulleys, he remembered

The fine hair of his newborn daughter
The smell of almonds on his wife's skin that first night
    together

He swells in goodness and peace till black pupils absorb
    his eyes as they close

Viaduct

Nothing in your horoscope could predict the time
When a woman removes her blouse to place your cock
    between her breasts

Now that's friendship

She is a grinning conspirator with tuning fork legs
And possibilities

She believes groping lovers practice vowel sounds
    in the dark
thus, fulfills a void

In his mind, he offered a silent prayer of gratitude as
    he told her,
"You are a victim of the things you sow."

Weather/Light

Consider fractured beauty
and skipping records of

Desire
Desire
Desire

Trapped by the weight of gravity

A smoking Yogi
discovers the power of flight
in velvet silence
on sinking stones

Whisper Song

In a place where Native Americans trekked to unknown land
pastures of ochre and green
I rode my bicycle along the Trail of Tears

A fallen monarch barely fluttered in the tepid breeze
This ancestor on a journey to Mexico
would herald the arrival of the dead
who returned to Earth

I placed the damaged monarch inside my blouse
close to my heart
It left a metallic residue on my finger tip
and made the sign of the cross upon my forehead

Like a modern-day Aztec,
I pedaled swiftly with reverence

What offerings does one make to a soul
whose journey is long and uncertain?

I offered sweet water
and protection for the travel ahead

The monarch heard my words
A prayer in an ancient tongue
I measured the slight movement on my finger
and swayed to a silent song

I positioned my compadre underneath a nest of violet
    red flowers
and mourned a story written in stone

Windowpane

Girls make out
with the boys who are forbidden and convincing
They know what it's like to run through cornfields in
Kansas
Naked
On acid

And the last names of the boys we loved
we attached to our own
scribbled over and over

Till all the names cover thousands of notebooks and papers
that end up in landfills the size of tiny men nations

Suppose you love men so much
that you begin thinking like them?
As one lover leaves another replaces him

Petroglyphs in Chaco Canyon are really ancient
porn symbols that translate to, "Yoo-hoo!"
like drinks that arrive at your table, "Yoo-hoo!"

Trees blink with tiny electrical bugs that live to mate
The man of the house thinks it's funny
to mimic patterns with the porch light off and on
thus endowing himself with the biggest light
The limping professor who swears he's Buddhist

pays literary tribute to women he has loved
In his ancient heart
desire and memories
suffer in prose, or in his right hand

A woman I know once wore sunglasses on a plane
and pretended to be deaf to avoid contact
till the end of the flight when she leaned over the cockpit
and thanked the pilot for the ride

Maria Vasquez Boyd is producer/host, of Artspeak Radio a weekly live program on 90.1FM KKFI Kansas City Community Radio. Since 2012, she features local and world renowned artists, writers, poets, playwrights locally and internationally. Boyd is a founding member of the Latino Writers Collective, a storyteller, poet, artist, designer, painter, and continues to exhibit her work across the country. She served as Poet in Residence for *Present Magazine* in Kansas City, Missouri.

www.ingramcontent.com/pod-product-compliance
Lightning Source LLC
Chambersburg PA
CBHW031255120626
46545CB00007B/2829